Times Square Everywhere

The Next Wave in the Fast-Changing Media Landscape

Times Square Everywhere

The Next Wave in the Fast-Changing Media Landscape

Mark A. Boidman

LEON SMITH
PUBLISHING
www.LeonSmithPublishing.com

ISBN: 978-1-945446-48-1

Acknowledgments

This book would not have been possible without the support and encouragement of my children, my parents, my brother, and Peter J. Solomon.

A special thank-you goes to PJ SOLOMON, Michael Blackburn, Christian Bermel, Diane Coffey, Christina Giliberti, Eric Lesorgen, Andrew Liou, Brandon Yoshimura, and Ben Zinder.

Contents

CHAPTER FIVE

Introduction

The media industry has changed dramatically during the last decade. Technology continues to impact the media channels that deliver content and advertising to consumers.

In this book, I explore how digital and mobile media are changing the media landscape. I illustrate for marketers the benefit of the out of home media channel and why it should not be overlooked.

I also discuss *out of home media* and the ways in which technology enhances the out of home media industry.

What is out of home media?

Out of home media, outside media, and *outside the home media* all refer to any media experienced outside your residence, including posters, billboards, screens, and displays seen in any of these locations:

- The back of taxi seats
- Taxi rooftop displays
- Elevators
- Gas stations
- Restaurants
- Doctors' offices
- Hospitals
- Museums

- Movie theaters (Cinema)
- Retail stores
- Shopping malls
- Sports arenas
- Hotel and office lobbies

Any sign or screen in the physical world not within your home is considered media outside the home.

I want to help you understand the implications of mobile media, consumption patterns, and how the media ecosystem is likely to evolve. You or your company can then be in a better position to take advantage of the evolving media and technology landscape.

Marketing managers would do well to give greater consideration to out of home media in their development and evaluation of a marketing mix. Many people still focus on the larger media formats or channels; they are unaware of the power of the out of home media channel, particularly as it relates to mobile and digital media and their impacts. Because the mobile generation receives and consumes media and content on the go, out of home media is uniquely positioned to be a leading media channel.

How will technology impact each media channel in the marketing discussion, particularly in the allocation of marketing and advertising dollars?

When marketers get together and talk about a marketing mix—be it web, radio, newspapers, TV, or magazines—

outdoor and out of home media tend to be at the bottom of the list. Given out of home media's unique characteristics and ability to influence consumers, it should be much higher in the marketing mix. It should be one of the first pieces included in a marketing plan, rather than one of the last.

It goes without saying that new technologies are impacting classic media channels, including newspapers and magazines, and making these channels less desired. At the same time, a number of technological challenges, such as web bots and ad blocking products, face the new media channels of online, video, and internet advertising. Web bots and ad blocking products make it more difficult to understand whether actual people are viewing content and advertising or fraud is occurring.

Technology has been a friend to only one media channel: out of home media. Out of home media is generally immune to fraudulent activity, and consumers don't have the ability to skip it or turn it off. In most cases, it can't be avoided by consumers. The ability to ignore, turn off, or skip ads simply does not exist in the physical world, both out of home and in retail stores.

My goal is to elevate the profile of out of home media as a media channel and inform investors, marketers, and consumers that this is a channel not to be overlooked. I expect this channel will grow rapidly over the next decade and quickly take a higher priority in the standard media mix.

The data presented here demonstrate the power of out of home media in the evolving media landscape. I mentioned fraud, for example. There are concrete data that show that most online ad impressions are not viewable or were not viewed by humans. In fact, in late 2014, Google reported more than half of online ads were not seen by actual web users.[1] One reason for this is ad blocking; many people are now activating ad blocking software on their devices so ads are often never seen. In 2016, more than 216 million global users were expected to use ad blocking software, up from 121 million users in 2014.

Please see the supporting data below:

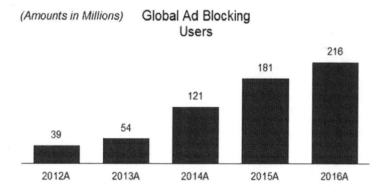

credit: PJ SOLOMON

Source: Pagefair (pagefair.com/downloads/2017/01/PageFair-2017-Adblock-Report.pdf, see page 5 of the link). "A" indicates actual results.

---

1   mediapost.com/publications/article/239523/more-than-56-of-ad-impressions-are-not-seen-goog.html

In addition to the impact of ad blocking on new media channels, fraud is rampant in online channels and many ads are viewed by bots, not humans. Because of this, marketers are forced to use other media channels to reach people. We see out of home media, a channel which cannot be blocked, benefiting from this need for accountability and true consumer engagement.

Retail technology, as I define it, includes in-store media and is synonymous with out of home media, except that it is media shared or displayed in stores. In most cases, retail technology does not display third-party content or advertising, but the store's content and advertising. For example, if you walk into a GAP store, you will see GAP's products promoted on screens or signage throughout the store.

The same goes for sports or entertainment venues. If, for example, you walk into a stadium, the displayed media ranges from content specifically related to what is happening onsite, like a team gift shop, to unassociated third-party content, news, or promotions.

My goal in this book is for you to gain an understanding of the out of home media industry and the retail technology industry, so that you can effectively leverage these channels as they evolve into two of the most powerful media channels of the future.

CHAPTER ONE

Technology's Impact on the Future of Advertising and Media

VARIETY OF MEDIA CHANNELS

Media channels and advertising channels are generally the same. With technological changes, the number and types of channels have changed over the last several years. Individual channels are grouped into two categories: *new* media, and *classic*, or *traditional* media channels.

Changing Number of Channels

Major classic media channels include:

- Radio
- Television
- Print (magazines and newspapers)
- Out of home

Radio and television channels are generally changing and shrinking.

Out of home advertising is changing as well, but in a positive way. For example, just seven years ago, dollars spent on newspaper advertising was about $21 billion. In 2016, that number was down to $14 billion. That is a dramatic drop in dollar volume for newspaper advertising. Magazine advertising has seen a similar trend. Seven years ago, it was close to $15 billion. Today, it's much closer to $13 billion.

($ in Billions) US Print Advertising Spending Historically

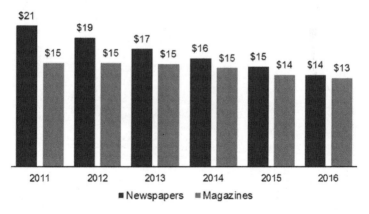

Credit: PJ SOLOMON
Source: Pew Research Center (journalism.org/media-indicators/digital-news-revenue-u-s-advertising-by-media/)

Of course, the formats for media consumption are changing as well. People consume television in a very different way today than they did five years ago, or even one year ago.

Because of that, the dollar volume of traditional television—also known as *linear television*—advertising has also shrunk. TV advertising growth today is largely associated with new media or over-the-top, nonlinear television, which I will describe in more detail below.

($ in Billions)   US TV Advertising Spending Historically

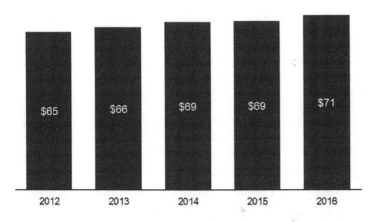

Credit: PJ SOLOMON

Source: Pew Research Center (journalism.org/media-indicators/digital-news-revenue-u-s-advertising-by-media/)

This stagnation of linear TV ad spend growth, combined with the dramatic decline in newspaper and magazine ad spending, will shift billions of dollars in terms of advertising spending away from these media channels.

But where is it all going?

Where are the newspapers and magazines advertising dollars being diverted?

Most resources are going toward what I call collectively the *digital media bucket:*

- Mobile and online video
- Display advertising
- Social media

As dollars shift out of the traditional, classic media channels into these new media channels, consumption patterns are also changing. For example, mobile ads did not exist in 2010; today, people are increasingly viewing them. By 2020, they will be the largest global ad segment. Just seven years ago, these ads barely existed. This channel growth represents a massive shift in advertising spending.

Defining Each Channel

Let's start with television, since that is one of the channels experiencing perhaps the most significant shift in how content is being distributed and consumed. Over time, this channel should be viewed simply as video, especially since, as corroborated by the Digital Placed Based Advertising Association (DPAA), video today is everywhere.

There used to be two ways of watching television: You could watch broadcast television—networks such as NBC, ABC, and CBS—or you could watch the cable network, which comprised channels that you could receive if you paid an additional fee for a subscription, such as Home and Garden Television, the Food Network, and CNN.

Today, people consume video in a variety of new ways with mobile devices and the internet. In addition to the development of new content channels, consumption patterns have changed from linear to nonlinear programming.

Nonlinear programming includes new ways to access television over an online or new media channel.

As examples, think of:

- Netflix
- Amazon Prime
- YouTube
- Hulu

These forms of nonlinear programming have changed advertising and media channels. They offer content in exchange for subscriptions and collect revenue outside of advertising dollars alone. They can also create *addressable advertising*, similar to the more targeted forms seen online. This advertising bucket will also change over time. The television bucket for advertising will start to shrink, as it should, or at least massively transform—from linear programming, broadcast networks, and cable networks to Amazon, YouTube, Hulu, or other new forms of nonlinear programming.

Some of the other channels, which I discuss later, are also facing the same kinds of shifts, thanks to technology. People consume those content channels in a different way. Out of home advertising used to consist of wall signs or static billboards. Today, there are digital screens, video content, and digital billboards. The out of home channel has evolved in a dramatic way because it can now show different types of content and advertising, depending on location, time of day, or weather, for example. Digital formats allow a number of variables to be considered in the display of content, making out of home media more impactful and dynamic.

The Impact of Digital

Now let's examine other media channels. Looking at new media channels, including social and mobile, these channels didn't exist ten years ago. Today, the social channel for advertising is close to $20 billion. Similarly, the dollar value for mobile advertising channels went from zero in 2008 to $60 billion in advertising spending in 2017.

Consider how these channels have grown: Mobile advertising has continued to expand rapidly. Companies such as Facebook are becoming more mobile focused as consumers shift to access Facebook and other online media channels while on the go. As a result, Facebook has changed the way they have relied on advertising to increasingly focus ad products on mobile advertising. That has dramatically changed the mobile ad bucket as well.

Other traditional channels—such as newspapers or magazines—are also trying to adapt to a new, digital world and are evolving their models to migrate their print legacy businesses online.

To recap, all traditional media categories— newspapers, magazines, radio, traditional or linear television, and out of home advertising—have been enormously impacted by technology. The impact for all but one has been negative; technology is only a true friend to out of home.

Technology has fragmented the audiences of newspapers, magazines, radio, and linear or classic television businesses. The only classic or traditional media channel that has done well with the development of media and technology and continues to aggregate a massive audience is out of home, and that is because technology has made the channel better and more flexible.

Digital formats have provided more flexibility and compelling content, and, with technology and mobile, out of home advertising's impact can be validated to prove that it is actually working. I explore that accountability in more detail in Chapter Three.

Mobile and online video are the largest growing advertising categories right now. This trend is expected to continue over the next several years. Again, out of home is the only classic medium expected to adapt well to technology and show real growth.

MARKET SIZE

In terms of *advertising spend*—revenue that is generated from advertising dollars—the United States spends the most. In 2016, the U.S. ad spend was close to $200 billion. The next biggest country is China, which spent about $75 billion USD.

The United States is by far the largest advertising market in the world.

Other countries that generate significant ad spend include:

- Japan
- United Kingdom
- Germany
- Brazil
- France
- South Korea
- Australia

All other countries engage in minimal advertising spending.

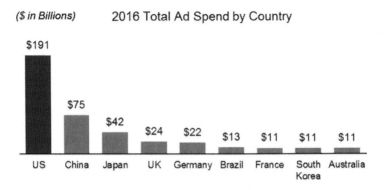

Credit: *PJ SOLOMON*

Source: Zenith Optimedia (zenithmedia.com/wp-content/uploads/2017/03/ Adspend-forecasts-June-2017-executive-summary.pdf)

Think about *penetration,* or the size of each channel compared to the overall advertising-spend pie. For example, of the $191 billion spent in the United States, out of home has about 4 percent penetration, meaning 4 percent of the $191 billion ad spend relates to out of home advertising. These percentages continue to shift as channels evolve. As such, the spend in each channel and penetration levels are also changing.

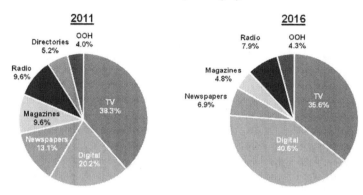

% of Total US Ad Spending by Medium

Source: Statista (statista.com/
statistics/272316/advertising-
spending-share-in-the-us-by-
media/

Source: MagnaGlobal, OAAA

How Total Expenditure Has Changed

In 2011, the out of home penetration number was 4 percent; in 2016, it was 4.3 percent. Consider the overall ad spend. These dollars of ad spend continue to rise, from approximately $160 billion in 2011 to about $191 billion in 2016. We can examine whether channels have maintained their share of the overall pie as ad spend shifts around.

Penetration

When looking at the above pie charts, you can see which channels maintain their share of the overall spend, which are growing their share, and which are shrinking. While some countries have shown a decrease in their overall ad spend during the last five years, the pool of advertising dollars, generally speaking, has increased. It's interesting to see that newspapers owned a roughly 13 percent share seven years ago and had 7 percent in 2016. These downward trends are particularly pronounced given that the overall advertising market is growing.

The data are telling: mobile, a nonexistent channel not even ten years ago, is growing quickly and taking share from many media channels. The dollar amounts have significantly shifted from classic, traditional media channels into these newer media channels.

Digital Dollars From Traditional Media Channels

The mobile channel has changed media, both from an advertising and a consumption perspective. The data clearly show that people are spending more time with mobile and digital media than ever before, which is changing consumption and advertising patterns.

Mobile extends beyond a way to consume content; it's an engagement tool, as well as a tool to make life easier and more productive. Today, people use their mobile phones to perform a range of tasks, from making restaurant reservations to online banking. In instances like these, people are not seeking media content, yet as they use mobile apps to carry out these tasks, they are exposed to advertising. Previously, you wouldn't be exposed to an ad while making a restaurant reservation. This activity is a shift in how people are consuming media and advertising content, which is well reflected in these advertising buckets, dollars, and penetration levels.

Digital and mobile media present increased opportunities for marketing channels because there are new ways to use digital within each channel, thereby enhancing them.

The benefits of digital and mobile are not simply achieved in the mobile and digital buckets, but to out of home as well, and the distinctions between channels begin to blur.

TECHNOLOGY IMPACTS MEDIA CHANNELS

Technology is changing the landscape of media channels because it blurs the nature and format of content delivery, including the way in which media can be bought and sold. The average person consumes more channels than ever before; there are also new forms of buying and selling advertising media that change how dollars are spent on these channels.

Time Spent

The time consumers spend with digital media has nearly doubled in the past couple of years. In the arena of nondigital media, time spent generally remains the same, although some sources report it is down slightly.

Time spent with mobile and online media obviously continues to rise rapidly.

How do you turn that into an opportunity?

Traditional media channels are trying to make themselves look and feel more digital. Some magazines have shifted entirely to mobile formats. Traditional media channels are still exploring whether they can switch to a digital format successfully, but the outcome of this transition remains uncertain.

People are spending more and more time outside their homes. According to the Outdoor Advertising Association of America (OAAA), people are spending 70 percent or more of their waking hours outside their homes. That creates a real opportunity for out of home media.

Innovation

Previously, television was the go-to advertising medium for companies wishing to promote their products to a broad audience. That is changing today because television's audience has fragmented and because other media channels continue to aggregate a mass audience, including out of home advertising, which also allows companies to reach targeted audiences.

Many of the traditional billboards that people are accustomed to seeing on highways are being replaced with digital billboards. Also, digital screens can display what I call a *Wow! creative,* meaning a *creative*—or advertising strategy—that stands out and is more appealing to the audience. This screen can also be contextually relevant—displaying the right advertisement or right content at the right time and in the right location.

Technology makes it possible now to show an advertisement for hot chocolate on a cold day, coffee in the morning, a movie in the evening, or an entertainment venue promoting an evening out on the town. There is opportunity to schedule advertising relevant to the time of day with media content.

Technology also allows for *smart cities,* or cities that gather information via electronic data collection sensors to improve and highlight city services and infrastructure. A smart city offers connection to the internet either through Wi-Fi or other technologies to provide services to consumers and solve urban problems.

Services include:

- Free Wi-Fi
- Smart trashcans
- Smart lighting systems
- Smart parking meters

This is a reflection of continued innovation through location-based technology, which is making a huge impact.

Mobile has also aggregated an audience. More than 85 percent of people in the United States now own or have ready access to a smartphone, and more than 70 percent of U.S. adults use social media.

Social media information allows advertisers to know where people have been, where they are now, and where they are going next. This knowledge is valuable to both content owners and advertisers because it allows them to advertise the right information to the right person at the right time and in the right location. Again, it allows advertisers to create highly targeted messages for consumers.

Consumer Engagement

With mobile phones, organizations can engage consumers throughout the day. In the physical world, this includes devices at kiosks. In certain venues—such as a cruise ship, a hotel lobby, or an office building—there are physical kiosks where you can browse on a device for contextually relevant information, in other words, nearby locations for any interest area, such as recreation, entertainment, or shopping.

At Twitter's headquarters, a massive screen allows you to peruse users' tweets. This provides an opportunity to engage with people in the physical world through digital devices.

If you want to make dinner reservations on a cruise ship, how powerful is it that you can do so from the screen in the lobby, or view a video and then book a related shore excursion?

All these advertisements increase consumption patterns of services, goods, and media content.

Doctors' offices and hospitals are perfect examples of what is changing with the advancement of technology. Many of the companies that provided patient education via the brochures on the walls of doctors' offices have digitized their content and the distribution of it. Many offices now employ digital screens in those locations. Patients can receive content, often sponsored by advertising.

In fact, *Point-of-Care Media* (POC) is one of the fastest growing sectors in healthcare education and media today. With the rapid proliferation of technology and digital screens across physician offices, pharmacies, and hospitals, the $500 million POC market has grown more than 10 percent annually over the last few years.

Because the majority of treatment decisions are made in these authoritative and trusted environments, POC advertising and content is uniquely positioned to reach a target audience, while facilitating more effective dialogue between patients and healthcare practitioners. A direct correlation between patient education and related healthcare follow-up action is already apparent, with multiple POC companies reporting material increases in vaccinations and other forms of preventive screenings, treatment, and procedures.

CHAPTER TWO

The Rise of Digital and Mobile Media

POPULARITY OF DIGITAL MEDIA

Every media channel today is having a harder time aggregating an audience. With digital fragmentation—a result of new technologies to distribute content and advertising, as I noted earlier—people spend more time with mobile devices. The result on the advertising side is an increase in supply—an almost infinite supply—of digital inventory is now available in the marketplace.

Digital and mobile media channels continue to increase rapidly in terms of usage and time spent per day. In comparison, minutes of usage per day in more traditional media channels are either holding steady or trending downward.

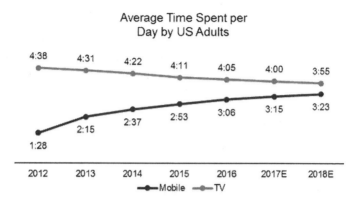

Average Time Spent per
Day by US Adults

Credit: PJ SOLOMON

Source: eMarketer (emarketer.com/Article/Growth-Time-Spent-with-Media-Slowing/1014042) "E" indicats estimated results.

Mobile Devices Mean Increased Exposure to Digital Media

People today research and plan their daily activities using mobile phones. Whether it's the daily journey to and from work, planning recreation time, or making purchases, planning is often done via mobile devices.

Mobile devices have become indispensable, essential, an absolute must-have. This has caused a dramatic change in the media industry. Initially, people were more comfortable watching TV and using their mobile phone or mobile device at the same time—the second screen concept. However, over the last several years, the mobile phone or the tablet has become the first screen, and the TV, if involved at all, has become secondary.

The real powers of any media are engagement and interaction. While television has been a classic channel, receiving a majority of advertising dollars, linear television programming offers consumers the opportunity to engage with neither content, nor advertising. You cannot click, touch, feel, or move traditional television media. It is a passive, lean-back experience. With mobile devices, as well as most digital out of home media, you can engage with the screen and interact with it. That has changed the landscape of media.

There are opportunities in specific locations to engage with media, which means increased exposure with that media. For example, while you are on the train, subway, or bus, you now have an opportunity to use a media device on the go. That gives you the ability to spend more time with media than in the previous decade.

The invention of larger-screen mobile devices, such as the iPad and other tablets, has changed the nature of media and the consumption of it. Larger devices have quickly risen in popularity because of the enhanced media display, including the larger format content.

Media Surrounds Us More Than Ever

The increase of exposure to media because of mobile devices goes beyond personal devices. Video is all around us—screens are now visible in places such as the gas pump, medical offices, highway billboards, and the sides of skyscrapers. Video is beyond the concept of television—a single, dated format. The Digital Place Based Advertising Association (DPAA) refers to this video domination as *video everywhere.*

Another avenue in which I expect to see more video delivered to consumers is via free Wi-Fi towers. These have been introduced in many public spaces, including the streets of several large cities. These Wi-Fi hubs are supported by digital ads, which run on the tower-like devices' screens. I expect more video content to be added to hubs like this throughout the world in the coming years.

Video has also made its way into retail stores, many of which have implemented screens playing videos that demonstrate a service or product onsite, such as in the GAP example noted in the introduction of this book. There are also info kiosks where shoppers can browse and select merchandise while in stores.

The out of home media technologies present onsite in retail stores constitute what I call the *retail tech market.* There, customers have the opportunity to engage with mobile devices in a powerful way. New technology brings advertising to shopping cart screens, shelf monitoring and shelf content, system screens at the point of sale, and screens in dressing rooms. There are all sorts of opportunities to engage with the consumer via newly developed media formats. This has made us more accustomed to seeing media everywhere.

In shopping malls and airports, there used to be simple, traditional, classic billboard poster advertisements, known as *directional advertising*. As media has evolved, the opportunity to have infinite amounts of advertising has transformed public places, allowing for a variety of dynamic and video content. Today, for example, when walking through an airport, in addition to seeing a screen directing you to your gate or terminal, you will see live news, airport information, media content, or advertising that improves your experience and is contextually relevant to where you are in the airport.

TIME SPENT WITH MOBILE MEDIA IS RAPIDLY INCREASING

Another area that is important to discuss is the personalization of content. Mobile media is more one-to-one, screen-to-person advertising; rather than one-to-many. In terms of personalized digital technology overall, mobile is superior because it allows content distribution that is contextually relevant to a physical location.

For example, if you are in a specific city or in a specific place within the city, digital content can be tailored to your location, and it can be interactive. These characteristics make it a better experience for a you as a consumer, with personalized content. Digital advertising is more relevant to you, and you will want to spend more time with that media to solve your problem or enhance your experience in that location.

I want to again touch on smart cities. Remember, smart cities are those that collect data and provide data to consumers on a secure network. As cities become smarter and roll out more media content, advertising, and information, that information is highly valuable. We are starting to see more of these technologies being deployed and the number of smart cities growing. This technology will also enhance the time people spend with mobile and content while they are in these smart cities.

More Mobile Than Ever Before

People are now more comfortable with having mobile devices and with being reachable while on the go. The Outdoor Advertising Association of America (OAAA) states that people spend 70 percent of their waking hours outside their homes. The fact that people are spending so much more time on the go, and are comfortable doing so, is because they have their phones with them. This evolution in consumer behavior connects to the smart cities opportunity.

If smart cities can provide connectivity and communications to the streets, as many cities are starting to do, they can also provide contextually relevant content and information throughout people's daily journeys from place to place. There are many companies that work with municipal governments and transit authorities to win the public's trust to provide secure information and media content in public places.

Previously, more than thirty million people would tune in to the premiere or series finale of a major television show. That doesn't happen anymore because there are so many different forms of media channels, ways to access programming, and ways to deliver and distribute content. If you want to reach a mass audience today, television is no longer the optimal distribution channel, as I discussed earlier. Eventually, it could be the streets of cities.

Rolling out media content and information that is contextually relevant is valuable to consumers. The more relevant the content is to users, the more attention they will give to it. They will not want to skip it or fast-forward through it. Frankly, they won't be afforded those options on city streets, which is another reason why I really support the opportunity for advertisers to use smart cities content and media to engage with consumers.

On-the-Go Engagement

It's optimal to reach consumers when they are on the go in *purchase mode,* also known as *action mode.* Action mode is very different from sitting on the couch watching television. When you are on the go in a public place and in action mode, you are more receptive to engaging with advertisements and subsequently more likely to make a purchase, especially if such purchase is contextually relevant.

Previously, brand-specific advertisements relevant to a specific location may have been a billboard that said:

TAKE THE NEXT EXIT FOR MCDONALD'S.

That is powerful. But there is now the opportunity to engage someone on a mobile device as they are walking down the street with a notification:

On the next corner, there is a McDonald's.

That is even more powerful advertising. Again, McDonald's fans want to receive that type of advertising because they are in that location, so it is contextually relevant—and welcomed.

People are willing to provide information, such as their location, in order to receive the type of tailored information that provides contextually relevant advertising. As I've said, seeing an ad on TV is very different because when you are sitting on the couch, watching television in your living room, you are not in action mode. For most people, that ad on TV is not relevant to them at that time and location.

As mentioned before, many people may view advertising as a potentially intrusive medium, and candidly, many are motivated to skip advertisements, click away, or try to avoid or block advertisements. When you encounter advertisements on public displays when you are in a public area, you can't skip them or pass over them. These advertisements are always on.

Younger Generations

Because young people have grown up with mobile, they expect everything to be interactive, and they expect everything to work. They want real-time, contextually relevant information. They also want and expect a fully digital, personal experience.

Imagine walking into a train station.

You're given information such as:

Hello, Mark,
Your train is arriving at track #7 at 8:30 a.m.

You would likely find such a heads-up valuable. If you haven't had your coffee that day, it would be pretty attractive to be alerted to whether a Starbucks is located in the station, and that, by the way, a new discount on Starbucks coffee is available.

Young people welcome this scenario. This is information they want to receive. These types of media programs win big with young people. Not surprisingly, young people are also highly receptive and increasingly willing to opt-in to programs that allow data-enabled digital screens to provide relevant content and advertising.

Again, this demographic has grown up surrounded by various forms of social media, and they are tremendously comfortable with it. They are less likely to be affected by privacy concerns. They're not disturbed by the idea of sharing data pertaining to where they have been or where they are going. Younger generations seem to be fine with that as long as data is anonymized and aggregated.

That is typically how most media owners and operators currently work; they are either aggregating data or anonymizing it. The key is for companies to articulate a clear privacy statement to their digital media users describing how the companies plan to use audience data and whether or not it is aggregated and anonymized.

AGGREGATING AN AUDIENCE TODAY

Previously, marketing officers operated under an ideology that television was the failsafe answer to advertising. If you chose television, you could reach your audience. If you chose something else and it didn't work, it was because you chose the wrong medium. Television was the foolproof channel, as evidenced by historical ad spend. Now, online new media channels are overpowering or are larger than the television-advertising silo or bucket.

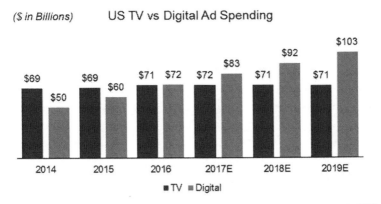

Source: Historical data from Pew Research Center (journalism.org/chart/ digital-news-revenue-u-s-advertising-by-media/) "E" indicates estimated results.

Television is no longer viewed as necessarily the best option both in terms of dollar spend and comfort level. Chief Marketing Officers can no longer depend on TV for their success. Today, digital media is providing that guarantee. People feel comfortable because of the attribution associated with online media channels, such as click-through rates.

The opportunity for out of home media to blend with mobile media is becoming increasingly important and relevant. Studies show that people are much more likely to engage with content or an advertisement on their mobile devices if they have first seen related advertisements or media content on a large screen in a public place. In fact, brands have demonstrated increased engagement of up to 60 percent when geo-temporal data was used in cross-platform campaigns.

Television

If a TV show today is successful, it's because it is reaching millions of people. Years ago, if somebody was watching a series finale, for example, *Seinfeld* or *M*A*S*H*, the audience for an event like that would reach 75 or 100 million people.

If you can no longer reach such a mass audience via television today, where do you go?

The answer is other media channels, where you can actually prove that you are reaching a targeted audience.

When advertising in doctors' offices or hospitals, you know you are reaching a specific consumer who may have a medical condition. You don't need to reach thirty million people; the audience is already selected and targeted. The advertising is as effective if you are only reaching a smaller portion of thirty million people, as long as it is the right audience. The contextually relevant, or more targeted audience, is more valuable in the mobile world.

Establishing a brand today through advertising is much more challenging because there are so many messages—thousands of messages a day. It has become incredibly difficult to stand out. That is another reason why I like spectacular forms of out of home media.

Spectacular is a term that is well known in out of home media. Spectacular media is found in iconic locations. It's dramatic, eye-catching, and situated in often high-profile or heavy-traffic public locations. I think this is the best form of out of home advertising because it is noticeable and always on. You can reach a mass audience in certain top national markets in these iconic locations, and you can provide them with contextually relevant content and advertising.

In high-traffic areas, with mobile phones collecting location data, a media operator can demonstrate with data that it is reaching an audience. With television, you may be reaching millions of people who tune in to a certain television program, but there is no guarantee they are watching the advertisements because of time-shifting DVRs (digital video recorders), previously known as *TiVo*. All the technologies that have hurt many of the classic media channels are helping out of home media channels.

There's no doubt that technology has negatively impacted linear or classic television advertising. With digital media and over-the-top programming, the ability to not see advertisements, or the ability to time-shift those ads, has hurt television channel efficacy.

Technology is a friend to the out of home media sector, and digital has only helped because, as I noted earlier, you can run different types of advertising throughout the day: coffee in the morning, and film or entertainment in the evening.

For younger people who have grown up amid the mobile revolution, a mobile media device has become the go-to device. Television is no longer the go-to device. Because of that, I think that television ad spend is going to continue to shrink over time, even with potential improvements—for example, over-the-top programming such as Netflix or YouTube. Even with over-the-top programming available on traditional television, you will still see audiences migrating to mobile devices. That will continue to put pressure on classic television advertising.

Television will continue to be a powerful media channel, but the way companies advertise on television will be different. The opportunity to run addressable or targeted advertising on television will certainly change television. Television advertising will become more engaging with the development of new media devices that make TV more interactive. Televisions are getting smarter with technology enhancements, making them more like mobile media. But mobile media is always going to be better than television, no matter how good or smart your television gets, because mobile will always be a more personalized, contextually relevant channel. All forms of mobile new media are going to be the go-to channel moving forward.

The challenge that television has, even with enhancements, is that it can't easily create a highly personalized, contextually relevant content experience for a consumer. The ability of mobile and digital media platforms to personalize content experiences has resulted in expanded share of wallet and primacy in the view of marketers globally.

Fragmenting Audiences

Most young people who listen to radio—or *audio,* as we like to call it now—in a vehicle or on their commute, have a very different sense of music in their mode of transport. When kids climb into the family car, they pull out their mobile devices to plug into the audio system of the vehicle or connect via Bluetooth technology. Their parents may want to tune in to the radio to listen to traffic and those young people find it comical because they are probably looking at Google Maps, Waze, or online traffic reports and getting live, real-time updates immediately. This very common scenario will continue to play out more often.

Traditional media channels are under pressure today. Radio, being a classic media channel, must figure out how to survive. Over time, the channel will change. Again, as an advertising medium, too many advertisements flood stations and the ears of users tuning into them. The only way to see success in radio is for advertising *spot loads*—thirty to sixty seconds reserved for advertisers—to be dramatically cut.

The challenge to doing this is that if you cut those spot loads and remove advertisements, the channel will lose revenue. As a result, I think many radio businesses will be under pressure until the right model is found because young people will continue to consume audio content differently from previous generations regardless of the classic radio spot load model.

With radio, audiences are fragmenting. Radio is just one example of a media channel's business model under pressure. For other channels, including magazines or newspapers, consumer habits are also changing.

Every year in our class for new analysts, we ask young people, "How many of you read a physical newspaper?"

Out of twenty analysts, *one* may pick up a physical newspaper. Everyone else gets their news online or on a mobile device. That is why audiences for newspapers are fragmenting.

Young people read the *New York Times* or the *Wall Street Journal* online or on mobile devices through third-party platforms; they increasingly don't visit the sites of these publications anymore. Younger generations have embraced curated news services. They are also reading content via links on Facebook and Twitter, which are personalized for them. That means that over time, the audience for newspapers will continue to fragment. Similar to the challenges facing the classic radio model, this classic media channel model is under pressure.

CHAPTER THREE

Out of Home Media

WHAT IS OUT OF HOME MEDIA?

Out of home media is any media displayed and consumed outside of the home. It comes in many formats. It can be defined broadly to include mobile media, which is media on mobile phones, because people often consume content on their mobile phones outside of their homes.

I like to use the phrase *classic out of home* instead of *traditional out of home* because *traditional* implies dinosaur-age media.

Classic out of home media includes:

- Billboards
- Street furniture (includes bus stands and shelters)

Out of home media also includes:

- Digital ad networks
- Digital out of home media
- Digital place-based media or screens

In summary, out of home media includes any physical location where there is a screen with media and advertising in public venues.

Out of home media can also be seen in private locations, for example:

- Office buildings
- Retail stores
- Restaurants

Categories of Out of Home Media

The categories vary primarily due to location and can include:

- Billboards—national and local
- Transit—airports, municipal, and non-municipal transit, taxis, and boats
- Point of care networks—screens or print advertising in doctors' offices, hospitals, or other venues related to or at the point of care
- Movie theaters
- Restaurants
- Bars and clubs
- Health clubs
- Offices
- Elevators
- Grocery stores
- Hotels
- Gas stations

- Shopping malls
- Retail stores
- Sports stadiums and arenas

As evidenced by the above list, there are several—and increasing—opportunities to engage with media outside of the home.

Some media experts refer to this method as out of home *advertising*. I like to define it as out of home *media* because there is a substantial amount of media outside of the home that is not advertising-focused or advertising-centric.

The category is even broad enough to include background music in retail stores designed to get shoppers in the mood to buy or create an experience in the shopping environment. I categorize background music within the retail technology industry. All forms of retail technology, in my view, blur with out of home media.

Retail technology includes:

- Background music
- Digital signage
- Point of sale media
- In-store kiosks

Retail technology also includes all media delivered via technology in-store.

Trends in Out of Home Media

As mentioned, the trend is that people are now spending more time outside the home and on the go because they can still remain connected via mobile devices. The ability to reach a consumer on the go is becoming more valuable. Out of home advertising spending has historically trended closely in line with the general economy. If the economy does well and gross domestic product (GDP) grows, out of home media and advertising budgets grow.

Over time, I see this format becoming less dependent on the economy because another driver of growth is *internet-connected digital media,* which is mostly supported by advertising. As more devices—including cars, machines, and infrastructure—are connected to the internet and the number of smart cities increase, out of home media revenue and advertising revenue will continue to grow.

As new technologies are created and more alternatives made available, the trend of out of home media options that allow for measurability, accountability, and attribution to prove it works will increase. When someone sees an advertisement in a public space and proceeds to make a purchase, this can be measured with information collected through mobile phones or a *proximity network.* I will describe proximity networks in more detail later in this chapter.

Out of Home Media, Retail Technology, Smart Cities, and Digital Signage

I define retail technology as the tools that allow for the deployment of advertising and content in retail locations. Retail locations can be stores, banks, and restaurants, for example.

Out of home media services in retail locations include:

- Background music
- Shelf monitoring
- Inventory management
- Shopping cart and dressing room technologies
- Audio or visual advertising

Screens and other media are growing throughout retail establishments.

You may have already experienced walking into a dressing room and interacting with a kiosk or screen. The ability to use augmented reality and other technologies to enhance the shopping experience is all retail tech.

The retail experience is also enhanced to level the playing field with e-commerce and online shopping due to:

- Point-of-sale systems
- Store management
- Digital and interactive displays

Some of the most impactful types of technology that overlap out of home media and advertising with retail tech and smart cities are *location analytics* and *proximity marketing*. They occur in both out of home media and in-store media. There is a huge overlap in these channels of technologies and vendors. Many of the companies that provide software to out of home media companies are also providing hardware and software in stores and in smart cities.

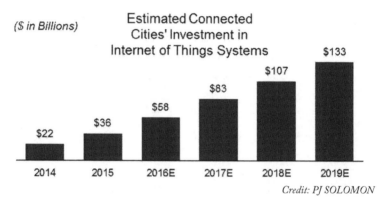

($ in Billions)

Estimated Connected Cities' Investment in Internet of Things Systems

2014	2015	2016E	2017E	2018E	2019E
$22	$36	$58	$83	$107	$133

Credit: PJ SOLOMON

Source: The Smart Cities Report (October 2016), BI Intelligence (businessinsider.com/the-smart-cities-report-driving-factors-of-development-top-use-cases-and-market-challenges-for-smart-cities-around-the-world-2016-10) "E" indicates estimated results.

What is the difference between out of home advertising and out of home media? There are a variety of formats of out of home media, but out of home advertising primarily reflects spend of third-party advertising dollars that is usually net of an agency commission, production costs, and any discounts. That is generally how you calculate out of home advertising revenues.

In terms of out of home media, using the prior example of a GAP store, GAP content will be displayed, potentially in addition to advertising on in-store screens. The content is the store's own media content. I define that as retail technology spend because there are no third-party media dollars being spent there. In summary, we don't define that as out of home advertising because it's not third-party advertising.

On the other hand, GAP's advertising on a screen in the concourse area of a shopping mall *is* considered third-party advertising on that mall's network, which would be part of out of home advertising spend.

INTERSECTION OF OUT OF HOME MEDIA

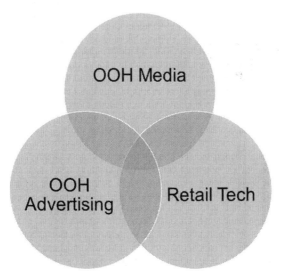

Credit: PJ SOLOMON

INNOVATION IN OUT OF HOME MEDIA

Technology is a friend to out of home media. I touched on this in prior chapters, but conversely, technology has not necessarily been a friend to the classic media platforms of television, newspapers, magazines, and radio.

As technology has evolved, the newspaper and print media industry has hemorrhaged. In stark contrast to this, classic displays or signs that have been digitized, and physical out of home structures that have similarly transformed, have stayed buoyant and flourished. We've seen growth in revenues and enhancements to the media content due to the ability to design more dynamic and eye-catching ads.

New digital media possibilities have elevated the industry, and this is evident in new screens in airports, within subway stations and on subway cars, within shopping malls, throughout entertainment venues, and in hospitals and doctors' offices. Digital media innovation is enhancing the quality of out of home media, and upgraded locations are enhanced with contextually relevant information depending on the location, its characteristics, and the time of day. That information is targeting a consumer who is, as a result of the content, better informed in those locations. The consumer experience in physical locations is enhanced because of the information and the media content displayed using digital out of home media.

Technology Is a Friend

As I described, technology has allowed the OOH industry to improve itself, while other media channels have been pressured by new formats and consumer channel shift. But the real value in out of home is not only from enhanced advertising and the ability to provide contextually relevant content, it's also because new technologies allow for measurement of out of home. As a result, it is more accountable since companies can now measure out of home media advertising impact.

In the old days, they used to measure outdoor ads using technologies where they put a set of glasses on someone's head and monitored their eye movements, or through monitoring the streets with a traffic sensor strip to count how many vehicles drove on a specific road.

Today, it's completely different. Out of home media is monitored by people's mobile phones. Advertisers are able to track how many people saw a display, how long they were there, and how often they are there.

Are they there once a day?

Twice a day?

How long did they spend in front of the screen?

Where did they go next?

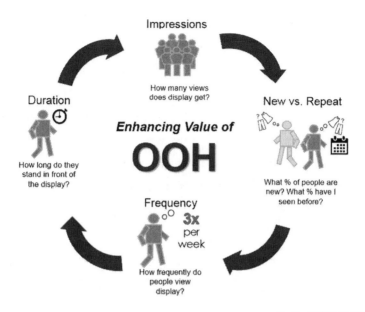

Credit: PJ SOLOMON

That is all very powerful data. Again, it's being driven by mobile phone usage because media owners use mobile phones to improve measurability.

Next is targeting. With mobile phones and knowing who is where, the out of home media companies are aggregating audiences. It does not report *Mark Boidman was in front of this sign,* but it groups people together into demographics with the right advertising at the right time. It reports *one hundred males, age thirty-five to forty-five were in front of the sign on Wednesday at 5:00 p.m.* Knowing the demographics means media owners can target their audience. It levels the playing field with the online world's ability to target specific consumers. Out of home media using mobile and location data can now accomplish this targeting in the physical world.

In my opinion, out of home media is superior to online advertising because there is reduced risk of fraud. Fraud is a huge concern online—bots clicking on advertisements instead of humans. In the physical world, there are no bots viewing billboards. Out of home media also can't be skipped in the physical world. You can't click out of it or watch three seconds and skip the rest. It's there, and it's much more readily expected and appreciated in the physical world because it provides information. Additionally, it enhances experiences while consumers are in action mode, potentially even on the path to making a purchase.

Growth of Formats and Technologies

Technology has a positive impact on the ability to employ and offer interactive advertising and interactive media content. For example, as I noted earlier, a doctor can guide a patient through an anatomical diagram of a heart or a brain on an interactive screen. The screen may or may not be sponsored by interactive advertising, but either way, the ability to offer this form of media and provide this experience is invaluable.

Additionally, high quality, massive, and spectacular digital displays enhance physical retail and street locations. Providing contextually relevant information and dynamic and engaging content is changing the retail technology and out of home media industries. Again, this is why technology is a friend to out of home media versus the other classic media channels, which are not benefiting from technology-driven opportunities.

Another opportunity is the ability to provide relevant information on a one-to-one basis, for example, in airports. Out of home media has traditionally been a one-to-many format, as in a sign displaying generic content for the many people who walk by. With mobile phones and proximity marketing, there is now the ability to push messages to you specifically as you walk through an area of the airport. If your flight is delayed or has changed gates, you may be messaged based on where you are in the airport, thanks to out of home media. That is pretty powerful.

This sequence can work in the reverse as well and become a two-way information exchange. If I am running to my flight and I pass certain locations in the airport, a gate agent, for example, can know with absolute certainty how close I am to the gate.

Should they hold the door another thirty seconds because I am just around the corner?

Or, am I five minutes away and they need to leave without me?

Digital displays with the right technologies make airports more efficient and demonstrate another practical use of out of home media and technology.

Growth Through Digital Signage

British Airways used spectacular digital signage in physical locations with billboard screens that had sensors. The billboards, with the British Airways logo prominently displayed, showed a picture of a small child looking toward the sky.

When the sensors picked up a British Airways aircraft flying by, the image would change to show the child pointing up in line with the aircraft and a message would appear with the real-time flight and number:

LOOK, IT'S FLIGHT BA341 FROM BARCELONA.

This was a unique out of home advertising campaign using a form of location-based technology to track the airplanes overhead.

The campaign, named *The Magic of Flying,* depended on a complex technological structure in which the billboard had to identify an aircraft's location, speed, and altitude, and subsequently create a virtual tripwire in order to display the British Airways advertisement at the correct moment. Additionally, the billboards were outfitted with capabilities such as detecting if it was too cloudy for the audience to actually see the planes.

Location-based media can also be used to provide specific information to consumers relative to consumers' physical locations, whether they are near an airport or shopping mall.

For example, location-based media could be used for a pet owner. A pet store could track weather and your physical location.

When you walk your dog past the pet store on a cold morning, store owners could leverage this technology to be able to send you a message that says:

> Hey Mark,
> Did you get your dog a winter coat?
> Go upstairs on the second level to see our best selection and new arrivals.

That is marketing information targeted to a relevant consumer, providing them with information that is topical and helpful.

It could be argued by some that this form of targeting is intrusive or gives the impression one is being watched. However, surveys reveal that millennials and younger generations are confident and comfortable with their information being shared or tracked—as long as it is aggregated and somewhat anonymous. They would prefer to receive the information, discounts, or other opportunities that will help them personally.

In a 2017 YouGov survey, only 31 percent of consumers said they would not be willing to share personal data for benefits; the remaining 69 percent responded that they would be happy to share their data in exchange for promotions, discounts, recommendations, and other information.

While it may seem intrusive to some that digital media tracks your location to provide you personally with the best media content and advertising available, others find it beneficial, particularly if it is solving an urban problem in a smart city.

Digital out of home media and billboards are growing, with close to double-digit compound annual growth rates in the United States. New digital screens—whether digital billboards or digital out of home ad networks—are growing close to or at double-digit growth rates year after year as well. Again, for a more classic media channel, these growth rates are quite nice to see, but not surprising in light of the discussion around technology's positive impact on out of home media.

The cost of these displays has come down significantly. More static advertising companies are rolling out digital inventory or digital signage and screens. Different sizes of displays are becoming more prominent. Many companies, especially out of home operators, are rolling out smaller, street-level displays because of the lower cost and accessibility for pedestrians. Engaging pedestrians with poster-sized screens is quite efficient.

THE GROWING ROLE OF MOBILE

The ability for mobile phones to enhance out of home media is significant. Mobile phones provide out of home media companies with data gathering and measurement and information for advertisers or content providers. Mobile phones also provide the ability to engage with consumers in the physical world.

We can use mobile phones to engage with consumers or retarget them with a mobile ad. A 2017 Nielsen study revealed that out of home media is most effective in driving online activity. Other out of home media company studies show the benefits of sending an ad on a mobile phone when a consumer has already seen the advertisement on a billboard. There are data indicating as high as an 80 percent lift in sales related to this kind of engagement, whereas out of home media companies have indicated that the increase in sales tends to be approximately 50 percent.

In any case, consumers are more likely to engage with advertisements on their mobile phones if they have seen them already on billboards or in physical locations. Out of home media companies are comfortable pitching mobile advertising to clients. We will continue to see the out of home media channel and the mobile channel blur further as advertisers see the power of putting these two channels together.

A number of parallels can be drawn between out of home and internet advertising. Whether it's through web cookies or other measures, online advertisers can track sites you visit on the internet and send you relevant advertising.

With mobile and out of home media, advertisers are able to do the same thing in the physical world:

- Track where you are
- Track where you have been
- Predict where you are going next

Using all these data, they are able to provide you with advertising, which, in my view, is actually more powerful than internet content because in the physical world, you are on the go, you are in purchase mode, and you are much more likely to purchase something if you are out and about, as compared with sitting in front of your computer.

Another similarity comes from *programmatic buying and selling*.

What is programmatic?

It means an automated buying platform. Instead of having to speak to someone to buy or sell outdoor media, you are able to use an online advertising exchange to buy or sell out of home advertising. I think the future of out of home media lies with the ability to buy or sell this medium efficiently without human interaction.

Removal of friction around buying and selling out of home media is another huge opportunity for growth with this form of advertising. Mobile will also help drive this opportunity.

If you pass a large-screen billboard as you are driving on a certain route, you see the screen and think it's powerful and you want to buy that space right now for your ad—how powerful would it be if you could just purchase your advertisement right then and there?

And, have your ad immediately go on display?

That is the power that programmatic buying could bring to this industry.

Enhancing Advertising Execution and Enabling Interaction

Out of home media can create content that engages the consumer. I talked about the opportunity to engage with physical screens.

But if someone is waiting at a bus stop and has a fifteen- or twenty-minute wait, how powerful would it be if there were screens that allowed them to carry out a task, such as grocery shopping?

There are many cases in which grocery stores are able to put their content on a screen, and people are able to use the screen as a shop window to purchase what they need, then have it delivered to their home later that day. That is a compelling use of a consumer's *dwell time* waiting at the bus stop.

Mobile and out of home media also integrate with the opportunity to access content from television channels or content channels across Wi-Fi–enabled screens in the physical world on buses and other modes of transportation. Some buses now have Wi-Fi–enabled screens that provide information, news, and content that can be further accessed on your smartphone. If you are a passenger on that bus, you can take that content with you on your mobile device.

Couple that with location-based data, and it becomes easy to measure the return on ad spend. That is pretty powerful, pushing content and promotions and engaging with advertising.

We have learned that when consumers search or shop within thirty minutes of seeing an out of home ad, they are more likely to go online with a mobile device. This proves the power of combining digital signs with location-based mobile technology.

Someone sees an advertisement while traveling through a geo-fenced area, then a similar ad appears on their phone. They subsequently are much more likely to engage with the content on their phone. Placement and timing of advertisements have the potential to amplify and extend brand engagement to levels never seen before, again bridging physical and mobile media.

Mobile Devices for Retargeting

One form of mobile ad retargeting is the ability to have a mobile ad appear on your phone that you have already been exposed to in the physical world. Let's talk through an example of that. If you are in a restaurant and you are using a digital screen, such as an ordering kiosk, and you happen to see a brand of chocolate syrup that is going to be included in the milkshake you are ordering, the brand then uses that data to retarget you the next time you are in the grocery store. This way, when you walk by that syrup display, the brand can send you a note, information, or provide you with a discount to purchase it. You've seen it before, you've tasted it before—you've experienced it. Bridging the physical and the digital worlds with mobile ad retargeting is key because it's that retargeted ad when you are in the physical world at the right location that is actually going to call you to action to make that purchase.

Additionally, if you happen to see an advertisement for a movie on a billboard screen or even on a static billboard in a geo-fenced area, advertisers know you have passed by that billboard. Later that day, as you are surfing the internet on your mobile phone, advertisers are able to retarget you with an ad for the same movie. Again, having seen the ad already in the physical world and then seeing it on your mobile phone, you are much more likely to engage with it.

Measuring Out of Home Audiences

Geo-filtered ads delivered to a large audience with real analytics provide physical *attribution modeling.*

What does that all mean?

It means that OOH operators are able to use location-based data to prove that the advertising works. If you have seen an advertisement for a movie on a mobile phone or on a display in the physical world, and thereafter you walk into a movie theater, the media owner can prove the advertising works. That is attribution modeling.

As another example of that, let's say you're standing at the bus stop. You see an advertisement for shoes. The media owner is able to measure that you were there through beacons or other proximity or location-based marketing technologies, and then, because similar technology is enabled at the shoe store, they can measure that you went from the bus stop to the shoe store. They are able to prove to the advertiser that the advertising at the bus stop works.

What will be even more convincing down the road is the measurement of purchases. Let's say you see an advertisement for shoes at the bus stop. Then, you go to the shoe store and purchase the shoes. As your mobile payment is registered, the media owner will be able to fully close the loop and report: *This consumer saw the advertisement at the bus stop, went to the shoe store, and made a purchase using their mobile phone or a credit card linked to the phone.* This closes the loop for the media owner to prove to the advertiser that the advertising works.

By using your IP address on your phone, beacons, or other technology to create proximity networks, media owners and location-based marketing companies can measure how many people are in a physical location.

CHAPTER FOUR

Retail Technology

RETAIL TECHNOLOGY AND IN-STORE MEDIA

Retail technology, or retail tech, is simply technology and media, both in-store or in any other retail environment that enhances the shopping experience. It could be in stores; it could be in restaurants, which is food retail tech; or it could be in environments where there are retail applications, such as cruise ships, subway stations, and shopping malls. Retail technology is also referred to as *in-store technology* and *media*. Digital signage is a large component of retail technology.

Defining Retail Technology

Technology in the retail sector comprises a small part of the much broader technology universe. Globally, retail technology was approximately a $27 billion sector in 2015; I anticipate this growing aggressively over the next four years, getting to be as high as $45 billion by 2019. Today, digital signage is about a $20 billion industry globally, and that is likely to rise to just over $25 billion by 2019.

Retail technology includes:

- Background music or music systems in-store
- Digital signage, including digital menu boards
- In-store media
- Inventory management
- Kiosks
- Point of sale technologies
- Ratings and receipts
- Shelf monitoring
- Shopping cart technology
- Store management
- Wi-Fi
- Location analytics and proximity marketing

These are all areas of retail technology that are growing much bigger because of mobile technologies.

Out of home media is third-party advertising, or paid media advertising, and media revenue. For example, third-party advertising in a coffee shop would be out of home advertising.

Retail tech, as I define it, is almost the same thing. For example, in that same coffee shop, there is a screen that displays a digital menu of items you can order. Or, perhaps that screen displays an advertisement for the coffee shop's special coffees of the day. Digital menu boards form part of retail technology, even if there are no third-party ads or third-party media revenues.

Video content on that coffee shop screen that is not related to the coffee shop would be out of home media.

What if it's video content relating to how the coffee shop makes its coffee?

I consider in-store media to be in the retail technology bucket since that is not third-party video content.

Digital Signage Hardware and Software

The digital signage hardware and software markets are growing quite quickly. Digital signage revenue in the United States, in terms of equipment, software, services, plus digital signage media revenue, today is about a $20 billion market opportunity, using estimates based on publicly available data. That $20 billion includes about $7 billion of media revenue. Taking the media revenue out of the equation leaves roughly $13 billion for equipment, software, and services.

($ in Billions)	2014A	2015A	2016A	2017E	2018E	2019E	2020E
Displays	$6.7	$6.4	$7.4	$7.8	$8.5	$9.7	$10.9
Media Players, PC, & Set-Top Boxes	0.8	1.2	1.2	2.0	2.2	2.3	2.3
Software for Networked Digital Signage	0.3	0.3	0.4	0.3	0.4	0.5	0.6
Other Digital Signage Products	0.9	0.9	1.1	1.3	1.5	1.6	2.0
Services	1.8	1.9	2.3	2.0	2.1	2.2	2.3
Media Revenue	5.1	5.6	6.2	7.1	7.6	9.2	10.8
Total	**$15.6**	**$16.3**	**$18.6**	**$20.5**	**$22.3**	**$25.5**	**$28.9**

Credit: PJ SOLOMON

Source: IHS, "A" indicates actual results. "E" indicates estimated results.

This market includes hardware and software installed in physical locations, including:

- Retail environments
- Hospitals
- Medical offices
- Shopping malls
- Cinemas and theaters
- Transit locations

Digital media on screens in public venues reaches more customers than videos on the internet or Facebook. It's a pretty powerful statement of the size and scale of digital billboards and digital screens. The cost of rolling out a digital signage network continues to fall annually by more than 10 percent, and signage penetration across physical locations increases.

In addition to costs coming down, the number of *use cases*—or examples—has increased. Digital menu boards in physical locations, such as quick-service restaurants or coffee shops, are all being converted to digital screens. Menu boards are becoming digital menu boards. Even buffet table displays or paper tags at café food stations are becoming digital screens.

Cruise ships and hotel buffet displays are well positioned for digital. This is a huge market opportunity. But the opportunity extends beyond these use cases. A lot of these coffee shops and retail stores want to roll out massive screens right in the entry of their stores to create experiences and shopping environments in the store that level the playing field with online shopping. That is why more spectacular displays are being rolled out, especially as technology costs to deploy digital signage and retail tech in general come down. Many big cities will one day look just like Times Square.

Credit: pixabay.com

Opportunity for Media Revenue

In addition to creating a compelling shopping environment or providing information, there is the opportunity to roll out media content. In the coffee shop example, the shop can realize revenue via third-party advertising, such as a trailer for an upcoming movie or products that go well with coffee, and whether or not they are sold in that store. There is huge opportunity for local businesses and national chains to obtain third-party media revenue to increase their own bottom line.

Retail technology consists of displays, which often can be interactive. It also includes tools that are behind the scenes, such as analytical tools and back office tools. For the purposes of this book, I focus on displays in the store's forefront or public, interactive, displays in retail environments.

TRENDS

Retail technology is growing quite quickly. Integrating new technologies is key to brick-and-mortar transformation and survival. It's brick-and-mortar retail's best chance to remain competitive with online shopping and e-commerce. Store formats are certain to change to incorporate many of the aforementioned technology trends in order to augment experiential, interactive shopping environments.

Creating Experiential Shopping Environments

Digital signage can help facilitate an *omnichannel shopping experience.*

What is an omnichannel shopping experience?

It means a shopping experience that extends across multiple channels:

- E-commerce or online
- Physical store
- Onboard an airplane or cruise ship

Omni-channel shopping experiences could be anywhere, and digital signage makes this possible:

1. Through digital screens and kiosks, consumers can research products before buying them, for example, before even entering a store.

2. Screen displays installed at shop windows or points of sale provide consumers with information about products and merchandise.

3. Shoppers can do research on their mobile phones, and then upon entering a store, digital signage onsite can include an associated call to action.

4. Finally, digital signage can help wrap the shopping experience with screens that allow shoppers to make a payment at kiosks or by using their mobile phones.

Now that I've defined the omnichannel shopping experience, what does it mean to create an experiential shopping environment?

It means transforming a physical retail environment into an experience and bringing the conveniences and advantages of online shopping to a bricks-and-mortar setting.

Consider what happens when you shop online: You have the ability to share and compare products with friends, or research prices and alternatives. When you are shopping in a store, you don't necessarily have the ability to do that.

But, if you have digital screens and technologies in place and incorporate mobile integration into these screens, a retailer can turn a physical classic shopping environment into an experience with similar attributes to online shopping.

To compete and contend with the ongoing migration of consumers to online and digital channels, providing this type of online experience in stores has become critically important for retailers. Taking it a step further, creating targeted, addressable advertising that is customizable to a specific person, based on their demographic and other data points, is also now key. Digital signage and its supporting technology are making this shift possible.

Interactive Displays

Imagine walking into a salon for your scheduled haircut. You check in via the screen at the counter by inputting your name and information. You can see how many people are ahead of you. You know when you're going to be called. If it looks like there's going to be a long wait, you can spend your time doing errands or shopping nearby. When the salon texts you that you're next, you can wrap up your other shopping and walk back to the salon.

These are all the advantages of touch technology that enable more engagement, which means more consumers are using that technology. It makes the whole shopping experience more efficient. Interactive displays are making shopping and the shopping experience more streamlined.

Services can all be facilitated by interaction and engagement. When you engage your consumers, especially when they are in purchase mode or at a point of sale, they are more likely to purchase. They are also more likely to have a better experience, which fosters return visits, recommendations to friends, and further enhanced experiences.

Smart Cities Opportunity

The smart cities opportunity for digital signage and retail technology is massive. Some sources say that smart cities represent a $1.5 trillion market opportunity. Others suggest it is much larger than $1.5 trillion. That's not just digital signage or media; it includes energy, transportation, infrastructure, and governance, as well as technology.

Remember, a smart city has a connected network so that services within the city, and products that are delivered within the city, are connected by the internet.

City services such as trash collection, street lighting, and parking meters can operate more efficiently if they are connected:

- Trash containers can indicate when they are almost full.

- Street lights can detect when it's raining during the day, so they turn on for public safety.

- Parking meters can alert people when their time is running low.

There are all sorts of opportunities for smarter technology to make a city better and more efficient.

Right now, there are only approximately thirty smart cities spread around Europe, North America, and Asia Pacific. That number should rise quite quickly in the next few years. There will be many more smart cities service providers in the future, offering management and compliance services and on-site consulting.

In addition to trash collection, lighting, and parking meters, connectivity could include meters on homes and electric meters on commercial buildings that check for power use or water use. With smart meters, the need for someone to visit each physical location and measure how much energy or water is being used can be eliminated because the information is collected remotely.

Companies that detect gunshots being fired in public areas are connecting to smart cities. These companies can locate nearby police and dispatch them to that location. These are all technologies that are reshaping cities.

A lot of these services are being powered by advertising.

How does New York City support rolling out free Wi-Fi in a connected network?

Through advertising.

In New York, London, and other parts of the United Kingdom, cities are beginning to roll out free, public Wi-Fi networks. Networks are secure and safe for city services and city vendors to integrate with those networks to provide what I call *connected city services* through the internet.

Retail will intersect significantly with smart cities. As cities get smarter with a free, secure Wi-Fi network, retail stores in these cities will be able to connect to that network as well, which will reshape how consumers shop. In fact, you may see a situation in which a screen on the outside of a shop window becomes the store—because you can use touch-screen technology to make the purchase right then and there. This will dramatically change how you shop.

You could shop on screens in subway stations and have the products delivered to your home that day or the next day. There may be interactive vending machines. There are companies incorporating vending machines into these public locations so they look like giant iPads or tablets. These vending machines are designed to provide media content, advertising, and products.

DIGITAL SIGNAGE

Digital signage makes a powerful statement in retail. We are starting to see more digital displays, including interactive displays, in retail. Transportation is an area in which the application of digital signage is growing steadily. Other areas that are growing are hospitality and healthcare.

Screens are being rolled out in medical offices and hospitals to provide directions, advertisements by pharmaceutical companies, local ads, and patient education. Additional growth areas for digital signage include outdoor sports venues, the lobbies of theaters, and during what is called *pre-show cinema*.

Digital Signage Is Increasing

What is starting to happen in most retail stores, especially with young people, is that they are tuning out nondigital screens. They are so used to the digital screen in their pocket, and the ability to interact with those screens, that if they don't find that screen experience in a public store, they may not even walk in or feel comfortable shopping there. This dynamic is dramatically impacting how shopping malls and stores think and react today.

Within retail stores now, whether their products are clothes hanging on the wall or displays of food products, there are typically digital screens around or above those products. These digital screens showcase products, provide information, can be interactive, and even take the place of a salesperson to provide supplementary information. With interactive digital screens, you can determine if retailers have your size, the color you want, and make a request to have your choice brought to you.

Digital signage is driving sales and engaging customers, and the more you can engage with somebody at the point of sale and provide them with an improved shopping experience, the more likely you are to see increased brand awareness, as well as growth in sales.

More retail stores are deciding to spend money to roll out networks because it is no longer cost-prohibitive for them to do so. They also realize that networks are critical to create the experiential environment in the store necessary to provide a competitive advantage.

Capital Costs Continue to Decrease

The costs of hardware, software, tech support, installation, and even project management have all fallen significantly over the last decade, and they will continue to fall. Many companies overseas, particularly in China, have commoditized much of the digital signage in the hardware industry. There isn't a risk that the business will become completely commoditized because quality, reliability, and ease of use remain important.

Case-by-case decisions need to be made regarding where screens are purchased. It may be preferable to purchase from a company that produces low-cost screens in China; in other cases, you may need a technology interface that is proven because of its use case, and you require a higher-end, reliable, or easier to use technology.

In some areas, cost may continue to be a factor. Costs tend to be higher for the higher-end, custom digital signage products from the United States. Again, it all comes down to the use case, and you need to figure out on a case-by-case basis whether it makes sense to roll out a full-blown, connected, digital signage network, or whether what is needed are a few screens via a platform developed and manufactured overseas.

Lastly, although the expense of digital display hardware—and even software and tech support—continues to drop, there are different technologies being rolled out with hardware and software, such as beacons, Bluetooth sensors, augmented reality, and artificial intelligence. All these incremental technologies may add some costs in the short term, but they will provide a unique advantage for a one-stop-shop capability to connect with a consumer in a store.

Digital Media in Public Venues

As mentioned, consumers today are bombarded by 5,000-plus messages each day—some reports place this figure closer to 10,000. Either number is staggering, especially considering that consumers in the 1970s were exposed only to about 500 a day.

Amid this information overload, out of home media screens are standing out more than online advertisements, which stand out more than their television counterparts. Some surveys demonstrate that most people don't actually see online and television advertisements: more than 50 percent in the case of television and more than 70 percent in the case of online advertisements.

In a 2017 PJ Solomon Ad Recall Study, Out of Home Media, particularly digital out of home media, had the highest ad recall rate.

PJ SOLOMON AD RECALL STUDY

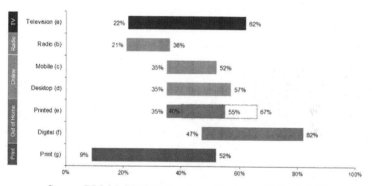

*Source: PJ SOLOMON Company Study as of March 2017
and Wall Street research.*
*Note: Ranges shift depending on aided vs. unaided recall basis, length of time
for recall, and sample size, nature and scope.*

a) *Includes linear and nonlinear television.*
b) *Includes terrestrial and nonterrestrial or streaming radio, including
either analog radio or digital audio over a variety of radio formats*

    (broadcast, simulcast, satellite radio, internet radio via streaming, media, on the internet).

c)   *Includes interactive and noninteractive banner ads that appear embedded in mobile websites, downloaded apps, or in mobile games on smartphones and tablets. Does not include text ads via short message service (SMS).*

d)   *Includes all forms of desktop display advertising on websites, including text, image, flash, video, and audio.*

e)   *Includes all forms of outdoor advertising, including billboards, posters, wallscapes, rotary programs, transit, airport advertising, and in retail venues. Dotted box indicates revenue-weighted composite of printed and digital out of home channels.*

f)   *Includes digital media used for marketing outside of the home and includes digital billboards, digital placed-based networks, digital signage, and theatre screens.*

g)   *Includes advertising in newspapers, magazines, directories, and circulars.*

If these statistics are accurate, I am confident that digital billboards—which cannot be skipped, blocked, disabled, or essentially avoided—are more potent than online advertising when focused on ad recall data. Out of home is distinct among the thousands of messages surrounding you every day. Today, for true recall, you need something that is memorable—something that has a strong *Wow!* factor, has strong media content, and won't interrupt your routine.

If you are on your mobile phone or tablet and there is an advertisement that comes your way, it may interrupt something that you are doing, or interrupt your routine and frustrate you. However, as you go about your day and you see a billboard or a digital screen in a public venue, it's less intrusive. I believe it's going to be much more accepted than a format that intrudes on your mobile phone experience.

Billboard advertising is also different and impactful. Because you are subjected to so many messages in a day, you may miss an advertisement on your mobile phone. A mobile screen will be too small for *wow!* factor. A large format screen or sign at the pedestrian level with contextually relevant content is more likely to be noticed and accepted. The fact that screens stand out and are contextually relevant contributes to digital screens in the physical world reaching more people than videos on the internet or Facebook. As mentioned, digital media is also reaching more consumers who are outside their homes in those public venues.

CHAPTER FIVE

Location-Based Data and Its Impact On Media

RETAIL TECHNOLOGY WITH LOCATION-BASED MOBILE TECHNOLOGY

As mentioned, the power of location-based data is becoming more pronounced in the physical world. Connecting that information with out of home media is making out of home advertising even more interesting. Think of smarter digital advertising options that are amplified by location-based technology.

Reaching Audiences With Location-Based Data

One of the biggest trends in both hardware and software is new forms of technological innovation. New tech features are being added into out of home advertising structures, as well as in-store systems. Proximity networks, or location-based marketing networks, are creating the ability to collect data from a consumer and message them either in a store or when they are on the go.

These technologies are developing predictive algorithms that allow media owners, or out of home media operators, as well as in-store operators, to collect information on the audiences that are viewing their screens, including:

- Demographic information
- Location of the consumer
- How much time the consumer has spent in that location
- Where they are likely to go next

As a result, the advertising and media content being delivered to audiences is much more relevant and has metrics that prove accountability to advertisers. It's powerful when we can determine the audience consists predominately of men and women of a particular age group. These and other parameters are making advertising more effective and efficient.

We can also use facial recognition software to monitor how long people stand to look at an advertisement in a specific location and capture data, including:

- What is the expression on their face?
- Are they smiling?
- Do they look sad?

Logging the reactions of consumers to content verifies for advertisers that their ads are turning heads. More important is the ability with these technologies to demonstrate attribution—that someone saw an advertisement and then made a purchase—which I will address later in this chapter.

Your mobile phone is providing location-based data. Cell phone carriers sell or provide such data to media operators, or to technology companies that provide such data to media operators.

Point of Sale

As I have mentioned, using data, advertisers are able to provide people with contextually relevant advertising in physical locations. As the OAAA has said, humans spend 70 percent of our waking hours outside of our home. There are many studies that show that when people are on the go and in action or purchase mode in physical locations, they are much more likely to buy something if they see an advertisement. That is the power of connecting people with out of home media.

When people are shopping in retail stores, arriving at the point of sale—traditionally the cash register, but today it can be a kiosk or self-checkout counter—there is an opportunity to engage consumers when they have their credit card, cash, or phone ready for payment. Placing an advertisement or a piece of valuable content in that location increases the likelihood of the consumer adding what is being advertised to their purchase.

New and forthcoming studies on this are significant. There is a huge advantage in capturing a consumer in purchase mode, even in their car. At a gas station, if you see a fast food restaurant ad on the screen at the pump, you are much more likely to then go to a fast food restaurant. It's much different when you see an advertisement for McDonald's while you are sitting on your couch at home. You are not in purchase mode; you are not on the go.

I define *point of sale* much more broadly than just being at the cash register. Obviously, there are degrees, but the cash register is as close to the point of sale as one can get in the physical world and getting somebody there is important. My view is somebody on the go, in purchase mode, on their daily journey is much more likely to consume than someone sitting in their office or someone sitting at home watching television.

Another example is advertising a sports drink at gas station pumps. Studies have demonstrated that people are much more likely to purchase that sports drink when they go inside to pay for their gas if they have just seen an ad for it at the gas pump.

We are starting to see the ability to retarget via mobile, which is an important point. With the gas station example, data can be collected so advertisers know you have seen the ad at the pump. The next time you happen to be in a convenience store, or a grocery store, or anywhere that sells that sports drink, marketers will then retarget you with another sports drink ad on your mobile phone. That is powerful because it reinforces the message you have already received at another point in time.

Opportunities to Reach Consumers

Today, companies are able to engage people with out of home advertising, whether in the backseat of a taxi, on a subway car, on the bus, on the train, or on billboards or screens along their daily journey.

Additional opportunities include:

- At the gas pump
- At a quick-service restaurant
- In the lobbies of office buildings
- In elevators
- In reception areas of businesses

For instance, someone traveling for work sees advertisements en route to the airport, in the cab they take to the airport, surrounding the airport, in the parking lot, in the shuttle from the parking lot to the terminal, in the airport, in the lounge, and then again in the seatback of the airplane. Constantly touching consumers on their daily journey with the same message is increasingly important because people receive so many messages during the day that they tend to block or ignore many of these messages, or they are lost in the volume of messages.

This is separate from all the messages they are receiving on their phones. That is why I believe messages in the physical world tend to stand out. There are data that say 90 percent of the people who walk into an elevator stare at the screens inside the elevator during the entire ride up or down. That is unique in terms of reaching both an audience and a consumer.

This is actually helpful because marketers need to think less about where they are going to reach consumers and more about when they are going to reach them, and the audience they will likely reach. Tying back into the purchase-mode point, my view is that *when* is just as important as *where,* and most important is the audience you reach.

Marketers look at when an audience is more likely to be on Twitter, when they are more likely to be on Facebook, and when they are more likely to be on email. That is all relevant, but my view is it is much more relevant to get somebody when they are in a mode of purchase.

One data point worth adding is that in terms of proximity marketing, which is the ability to reach people with a proximity network, if you think of a beacon network as a form of proximity network, there are data that suggest 300 million beacons will be deployed over the next few years. Today, there are probably 50 or 60 million deployed. That means that with beacons alone—which are not always the chosen or right proximity network technology—there is going to be a massive increase in the ability to reach a consumer with a proximity network.

To be clear, a *proximity network* is a network that is in close proximity to consumers that gives advertisers the ability to reach them and engage with them. It's the ability to reach somebody on a mobile device with media content and advertising. A *beacon network* is the ability to send messages to a consumer's mobile device in a physical location or track their movements.

ATTRIBUTION AND ENGAGEMENT

Until recently, the only real technology that efficiently proved advertising works was online shopping.

If somebody sees an advertisement, clicks on it, and makes a purchase; an advertiser or marketer can close the loop and conclude that the advertising worked.

With physical out of home media, people drive by a billboard or see an ad in an elevator.

How do you similarly close the loop on the attribution to know they actually made a purchase?

How can you prove attribution to confirm a person saw an advertisement in an elevator and it directly resulted in a purchase?

The advent of proximity marketing and new technologies that are using mobile phones to track consumer locations is addressing this marketer need. This is interesting: out of home media is now leveling the playing field with online shopping. I argue that it's even better because much of the response to advertising online is fraudulent. Advertisers cannot be sure if a real human clicked on the ad or if it was a robot or some other fraudulent click. Reaching and engaging with somebody in the physical world is, in my view, much more accountable, so the attribution is much more powerful than online attribution.

Attribution in out of home advertising should elevate out of home media higher in the marketing mix when evaluated against other media channels. It also makes out of home advertising a *strategic buy versus a tactical buy.* The distinction being a strategic buy is a core part of a marketing plan, whereas a tactical buy is a last minute or afterthought advertising purchase.

Location-Based and Other Technologies

The most important thing about a proximity network is the ability to connect with somebody and send them messages.

For example, a person could walk into a retail store, or a geo-fenced area, and receive a message on their phone that says:

Hey, did you know that [this product or service] is being offered a block from here?

That is targeted marketing because it's sending a specific message that is contextually relevant to a consumer.

This form of marketing is not without its challenges. The challenge is that not everybody wants to receive messages. My view is that if you can send somebody a message that is relevant to them or solves a problem for them, they will want to receive that message. But if you are sending people irrelevant messages all day through a proximity network, that has the risk of annoying the consumer.

It's one thing to be able to remind a consumer that a certain product or service they wish to consume is in their physical location. It's another thing to bombard them with various messages. You need to be delicate and contextually relevant. That balance is the challenge that marketers have today to help growing businesses.

Location-based technologies work to target and reach people in a store, but they could also reach people inside a geo-fenced area. You could have an area of a city that acts like a store, using beacons or other proximity networking technologies. You could set up a perimeter in a certain area, so, in essence, it would be a much larger store. Everything I have just said can work in a large physical environment, whether it's a park, an amusement park, a city block, or an entire city.

Knowing Who Visited a Store and Who Made a Purchase

With loyalty programs, stores are very interested in:

- Which shoppers are in their stores
- How much time shoppers spend in stores
- What parts of the stores shoppers visit
- How often shoppers are there

Technologies today let us answer these questions with absolute certainty. You can determine definitively who has been there and for how long. That is interesting to me, and I have been focused on this opportunity to monitor consumers and their consumption patterns.

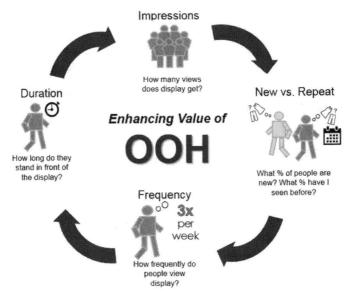

Credit: PJ SOLOMON

Engagement Enhances Marketing Impact

Whether it's at the point of sale or in a store, when a consumer is ready to make a purchase, they are much more likely to recognize advertising and to engage with it. There is huge emphasis on engagement today because when people receive more than 5,000 messages daily, successfully engaging a consumer with one of those messages is more likely to lead to them to remember the advertisement and compel them to follow through with a purchase. Engaged consumers are much more valuable from an advertising standpoint.

Many advertisers seem to like Facebook or other forms of online advertising because they provide an opportunity for engagement and an opportunity to hyper-target people. My view, however, is that if you can engage someone in purchase mode in the physical world, that engagement can be much more consequential.

When someone enters a physical location and you can track their behavior in that environment, it's powerful. Not only can you track impressions and how many views a display gets, but you can also track the behaviors the person exhibits in that physical location.

If you can measure the number of people who are exposed to an ad, subsequently visited a store, and made a purchase; then you have closed the loop, providing the full picture of the decision to purchase and offering something that advertisers will embrace.

Let's revisit my example of a consumer at a bus stop who is exposed to an advertisement for shoes on a bus stand or bus shelter. The consumer may also get an ad sent to their phone that retargets them based on the fact that the advertiser knew they were at that bus stop and saw the ad for that product. The consumer then goes to the store where that product is sold. The advertisers can measure through the consumer's mobile phone that they visited the store. That is proof that the advertisement worked. That is impressive.

Advertising can be purchased based on conversion on the basis of a *return on investment* (ROI), as opposed to some other form of pricing. Instead of paying a certain fixed amount per month to advertise on that piece of street furniture, advertisers can be charged based on proof that the advertisement drove people into their store and made purchases.

PROXIMITY MARKETING AND USE CASES

I discussed stores and shopping malls in relation to proximity marketing, which I have defined as the ability to engage with somebody in marketing at a physical location using mobile location technologies. Use cases can go much beyond that, however. Think, for example, of museums and parks.

At a museum, you as the marketer have the ability to use a proximity network to engage with somebody to say: *Since you are on the tour, would you like to receive content and information about the newest exhibit?*

If you're a visitor to a museum, a proximity network can track whether you have walked to a certain exhibit and send you a much more detailed level of information related to that exhibit than posters or tour guides could provide. The network could also send internet links that guide you to specific third-party websites that tie into the content of the museum.

Walking through a large park, you could receive the same sort of targeted information. Contextually relevant information about where you are in the park could be sent to you. Again, as a consumer who is walking through that park or visiting the museum, you are going to want that information because it will make your park experience or your museum tour much better while you are in that environment.

It's the same thing for sports and entertainment venues.

How nice would it be to be directed to your seat if you were lost in a large sports arena?

As you're searching, your mobile phone pings you with a message saying:

> **You are in the right area.**
> **Your seat is 9 rows down to the right.**

That is pretty powerful.

> The nearest food court is 100 feet
> from where you are standing.
> A special event is happening down the next corridor.

All that while you are in a sports venue is pretty interesting.

As mentioned, getting a message on your mobile phone about your upcoming flight would make your airport experience much more efficient. Of course, the ability to send you advertisements when you are in the airport is also powerful. Proximity marketing can be used in any physical location; I have just given you a few examples to illustrate its potential.

Businesses That Have Deployed Proximity Networks

A company called TouchTunes has approximately 65,000 jukeboxes across North America. They have created a social media proximity-marketing network so that when you walk into a physical location, they can send you a message saying:

> Check in on TouchTunes in this location.

Additional prompts will say:

> The following songs have been played at this location.
> Would you like to play your song?

Following these prompts, a user is then more likely to open the app and select music, transacting and viewing ads while doing so.

TouchTunes is the future of jukeboxes, or the now of jukeboxes, really. When I think of a jukebox, the image I see is an old-school jukebox with records in it. These machines, which were enormously popular and successful, are still around—but they've transformed into giant tablets installed on walls. You have the option to interact with them either at the screen, or on your phone.

The proximity network is made up of small devices that broadcast a distinct serial number over Bluetooth. When a TouchTunes mobile app user is at or near a venue with a TouchTunes proximity-enabled device, the TouchTunes mobile app will detect the signal. This allows for messages to be sent to the mobile app users that are designed to provide an enhanced app experience and, in turn, help to generate more user engagement and jukebox plays.

It's a pretty interesting use case for a proximity network. It's more than just getting somebody to purchase a product or service. In this case, they are purchasing music based on using that proximity network. Another jukebox company, AMI Entertainment, is exploring similar technologies to deploy proximity networks that will not only enhance music plays at venues, but also provide advertising and other marketing opportunities to tie jukeboxes to mobile phones and mobile phones to jukeboxes.

Other examples of proximity networks can be found in grocery stores. If you have a particular app, you could be guided to recipes and information. If you have a recipe on your phone, the app can then target you to walk through the grocery store to find all the ingredients you would need to purchase for the recipe. This represents another example of the power of proximity-network marketing in a physical location.

Collecting Data for Behavioral Insights

The ability to collect data on a person in a physical location is powerful for advertisers because it provides valuable demographic and other information. If you are going to advertise a new sports drink and your target audience is men and women aged fifteen to thirty-four, you are going to want to have accurate demographic information that says that in a particular physical location, the majority of consumers are fifteen to thirty-four.

Again, mobile phones, using facial recognition technology or not, have enough demographic information to prove to an advertiser that in specific physical locations, the right demographic is present. This provides a more accountable offering for advertisers.

This accountability used to be accomplished through surveys. Now, marketers can say with real certainty: *Based on all the mobile phone data we have collected in this location, your consumer is here.*

Advertisers feel much more comfortable when they have real, conclusive data. Mobile phone data provide the ability to say more than simply: *We think we are reaching your demographic;* advertisers know with certainty, supported by data, that they are reaching a targeted group of consumers.

This also relates back to that predictive algorithm regarding your location:

- Where you have been
- Where you are likely to go next

Again, consumer behaviors are being measured beyond just demographic information.

Sell Advertising Based on Proof of Performance

The typical way advertising is sold is on a *Cost Per Thousand,* or CPM basis. CPM is a marketing concept that means the price of advertising per one thousand impressions, for example, on a webpage or other screen.

MAJOR MEDIA CPM COMPARISON

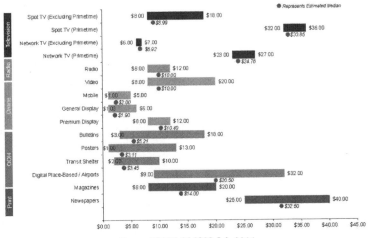

Source: PJ SOLOMON, July 2016

It could be $2 per magazine ad, $3 for out of home, and $10 for a specific mobile or online ad—there are different CPM rates per channel. On an ROI basis, you sell advertising based on sales lift. In my view, ROI-based is a much better form of sale because you are proving or demonstrating that the lift was there. In a grocery store, for example, if you see or hear an advertisement while in the store, the scanner data at the checkout counter will demonstrate whether the advertising provided any specific purchase lift.

I see this in healthcare practitioners' offices and hospitals where media owners price and sell advertising based on the demonstrated prescription lift. An advertiser promotes a pharmaceutical drug in a medical office that has a screen network with ads. They compare this setting to a control group in an office with no screens. A third party comes in and measures and compares the prescription lift between the two.

If both offices had similar prescriptions written before the ad network was added and the prescription lift rises for the doctor with the network, media owners can then demonstrate the advertising works, selling it on an ROI basis. That lift translates into a sale that is much more compelling than on a CPM basis.

You can use this performance-based model for anything. If you sell advertising for coffee on a screen in a café, once the network is up you can charge based on the lift in terms of how many more coffees are sold. This method is much more effective than estimating how many people are viewing or engaging with a screen.

The difference between CPM and ROI—and I think the aforementioned example illustrates this, but just to be clear— is on a CPM basis, rates are based on number of advertisement impressions, and ROI is proving to advertisers that they are actually getting their money's worth from advertising because corresponding purchases are made.

ROI demonstrates economic impact via attributed conversion versus an impression alone. It demonstrates economic impact via attributed conversion versus an impression alone. You are actually seeing the conversion, the purchase lift versus simply somebody's view of an ad. ROI doesn't always need to be tied to a purchase but could also relate to lift in the number of people walking into a store. That lift can be determined, and that's the value in ROI.

Programmatic Advertising—Technology's Answer to Mad Men

Programmatic advertising—using technology or software to buy and sell advertising in a more automated fashion—is certainly changing the advertising ecosystem. Programmatic technologies will further enhance the buying and selling of out of home advertising in addition to third-party advertising sold in retail stores. Real-time bidding on advertising and more efficient and automated buying is still being developed for out of home advertising. The playing field for out of home media will be further leveled with online advertising as ad buyers are able to buy out of home media from their living room at 2:00 a.m., just as they can do with online advertising. When out of home advertising in the physical world is as easily, or almost as easily, bought as online advertising is today, I expect to see significant growth in the demand for out of home advertising, and see it move up in the marketing mix discussion. Out of home is transitioning from an asset-based business to an audience-based business, which will be fulfilled through programmatic advertising.

Conclusion

The media ecosystem is undergoing a massive transformation that will change the competitive landscape of media and advertising channels, including how media owners reach consumers with content and advertising. Digital media—particularly the rise of mobile—will continue to impact the landscape and enable consumer interaction, allowing advertisers to efficiently deliver location-based, contextually relevant and tailored content and advertising to consumers both on and offline.

Out of home advertising today is a very small piece of the overall media spend in the United States—around 4 percent. I believe that this media and advertising channel is most likely to benefit from ongoing technological advances and transformation. As people are increasingly more mobile and on the go, the out of home media channel has a significant opportunity to benefit and increase its penetration. Out of home should show a substantial marketing mix penetration increase in the coming years, but even a few incremental percentage points from 4 percent to 6 or 7 percent of overall media spend would be a massive multi-billion dollar change for the U.S. out of home media industry.

Digital and mobile media will continue to develop as power players. The usage of both digital and mobile media is a real opportunity for out of home media.

Technology has been a friend to out of home, much more so than to newspapers, magazines, radio and other classic media channels. This competitive advantage is going to allow the out of home advertising industry to defend and take share of total advertising spend; something I am excited about.

Mobile technologies are making out of home media more accountable than ever before, using mobile phones to track how many people saw a display and for how long and for purposes of attribution to prove the advertising works.

The most important takeaways are to understand the benefits of digital signage and location-based mobile technology, and the ability of out of home to reach a consumer on the go. The benefits of the out of home media channel are numerous. As people spend more time with digital media, the opportunities continue to get greater in terms of reaching a mobile consumer with digital media while they are on the go and in purchase mode.

Companies are able to target and reach consumers at more points throughout their day using location-based data and out of home media. But the focus needs to be on a consumer's journey in addition to their location. I have talked about that in terms of a predictive algorithm and the importance of knowing where consumers have been, where they are, and where they're going next.

We need to recognize the ability to integrate mobile with out of home media. Those companies and countries that are rapidly integrating mobile with out of home are seeing real benefits. The United Kingdom, Australia, and other countries have pioneered mobile integration with out of home and are seeing material benefits from this work.

Across numerous cities, mobile is integrating with out of home. It's just a matter of time before we feel the excitement and energy of New York City's Times Square everywhere in the physical world.

Next Steps

I recommend attending the following industry conferences:

- DailyDOOH Investor Conference
- Digital Signage Expo
- DPAA Media Summit
- FEPE Congress
- London Digital Signage Week
- InfoComm
- New York Digital Signage Week
- NRF: Retail's Big Show
- OAAA/Geopath
- Out of Home: NOW (Advertising Club of New York)
- Shoptalk

I recommend joining the following trade associations:

- Digital Place Based Advertising Association (DPAA)
- Digital Signage Federation (DSF)
- Geopath
- Out of Home Advertising Association of America (OAAA)

About the Author

Mark Boidman is an investment banker in New York City. He has over eighteen years' experience in public and private mergers and acquisitions, divestitures, financings, private placements, and restructurings.

He advises companies across the media and technology sectors, including digital media and media services with a focus on out of home media, retail (in-store) media and technology, and mobile and has advised clients in industry-changing M&A transactions with a combined transaction value of over $40 billion.

Mark has been named to the *40 Under Forty* by the National Association of Certified Valuators and Analysts and the Consultants' Training Institute, *Investment Banking MD of the Year* by Corporate Vision Magazine's Executive Awards, and *Dealmaker of the Year* by *Business Worldwide* magazine.

Mark is a partner at PJ SOLOMON. Before joining SOLOMON, Mark was the head of Barclays (originally Lehman Brothers) out of home media, and TV broadcasting and radio coverage as a part of Barclays Global Technology, Media, and Telecom Group. At Lehman Brothers, Mark was in the Media M&A Group and a member of its Global Advisory Committee. Prior to Lehman Brothers, Mark was an attorney in the M&A Group at Paul, Weiss, Rifkind, Wharton & Garrison.

Mark received joint LLB and BCL degrees from the Faculty of Law at McGill University and is admitted to practice law in New York and Massachusetts. He also studied business at McGill's Faculty of Management and received the J. W. McConnell Scholarship. During his final year at McGill, he clerked for the Superior Court of Quebec.

Made in the USA
Middletown, DE
13 April 2018